NOV 0 5 2011

INDIANA
PACERS

by Josh Fowler

Printed in the United States of America,
North Mankato, Minnesota
062011
092011

 THIS BOOK CONTAINS AT LEAST 10% RECYCLED MATERIALS.

Editor: Chrös McDougall
Copy Editor: Anna Comstock
Series design and cover production: Christa Schneider
Interior production: Carol Castro

Photo Credits: Michael Conroy/AP Images, cover, 35, 44, 47; John Bazemore/AP Images, 1 L.M. Otero/AP Images, 4, 43 (middle); Bill Kostroun/AP Images, 6, 8; AP Images, 10, 13, 42 (top); Harrity/AP Images, 14; George Gojkovich/Getty Images, 17, 42 (middle); Lennox McLendon/AP Images, 18, 42 (bottom); JPF/AP Images, 21; Dick Raphael/NBAE/Getty Images, 23; Eric Risberg/AP Images, 25; David Scarbrough/AP Images, 26, 43 (top); Charles Kelly/AP Images, 28; Ron Frehm/AP Images, 31; Mark Lennihan/AP Images, 32; Darron Cummings/AP Images, 36, 39, 43 (bottom); Kathy Kmonicek/AP Images, 41

Library of Congress Cataloging-in-Publication Data
Fowler, Josh, 1986-
  Indiana Pacers / Josh Fowler.
    p. cm. -- (Inside the NBA)
  Includes index.
  ISBN 978-1-61783-159-1
  1. Indiana Pacers (Basketball team)--History--Juvenile literature. I. Title.
  GV885.52.I53F68 2012
  796.323'640977252--dc23
                        2011019673

TABLE OF CONTENTS

CHAPTER 1

BOOM, BABY!

The Indiana Pacers were in a familiar situation on May 7, 1995. It was Game 1 of the National Basketball Association (NBA) Eastern Conference semifinals. The Pacers were on the road at Madison Square Garden to face their archrivals, the New York Knicks.

The Knicks had knocked the Pacers out of the playoffs in each of the previous two years. Now, with 18.7 seconds remaining in Game 1, the Pacers trailed New York 105–99.

Following a timeout, guard Mark Jackson got set to inbound the ball for Indiana.

Pacers teammate Reggie Miller emerged from a cluster of players and received the pass on the left wing. He immediately turned and fired a three-pointer, rising just above Knicks guard John Starks.

"Boom, Baby!" Pacers broadcaster Bob "Slick" Leonard called as the ball went through

Pacers guard Reggie Miller puts up a three-pointer for three of his eight points in nine seconds in Game 1 of the 1995 Eastern Conference semifinals.

Mark Jackson, *left,* and Reggie Miller taunt New York Knicks fans during the Pacers' 107–105 comeback win in the 1995 playoffs.

the hoop. The Knicks' lead had shrunk to 105–102 with 16.4 seconds to go.

Anthony Mason went to inbound the ball for the Knicks. But he could not find an open man. Flustered, Mason pushed his pass toward teammate Greg Anthony. But as Mason let go, Anthony fell to the floor. Pacers guards Byron Scott and Miller had been guarding him tightly. When Anthony fell, Miller threw his hands in the air to claim innocence. Then he saw the ball and immediately snatched it out of the air.

Knowing his team was down by three points, Miller turned around, dribbled once, and set up his shot behind the three-point arc. Anthony's outstretched arm obstructed Miller's vision. But it was to no avail. The net barely moved as Miller's game-tying shot swished through the hoop with 13.2 seconds to play.

"Oh he threw it away!" Leonard yelled. "Reggie for three! Boom, Baby! It's a tie ballgame! Unbelievable!"

The Pacers momentum briefly halted when forward Sam Mitchell committed an away-from-the-ball foul on Starks. The Knicks' guard went to the free-throw line.

Starks's first attempt rattled out. A capacity crowd gasped. Starks took the ball from the referee and hoisted up his second attempt. The ball hit the front iron of the rim and bounced back into play.

Knicks center Patrick Ewing grabbed the rebound, but his jump shot missed as well. This time, the ball landed in the hands of Miller. He was immediately fouled.

Miller had missed some crucial free throws against the Knicks the year before. But he soon made up for that. With his robot-like precision, his first free throw dropped straight through the basket: 106–105. His second free throw was a mirror image of the first. It put the Pacers up 107–105.

A Heated Rivalry

Between 1993 and 2000, the Indiana Pacers and the New York Knicks met 35 times over six postseason series—the most of any two teams during that time. This created one of the fiercest NBA rivalries of the 1990s. The Pacers won 18 of those games; the Knicks won 17. Series victories were even at three apiece. Against the Knicks in the playoffs, Pacers star Reggie Miller averaged 23.1 points per game—nearly five points above his career average during the regular season (18.2) and nearly three points higher than his career playoff average (20.6).

Reggie Miller and the Pacers finally beat the New York Knicks in a playoff series with their victory in 1995.

With less than eight seconds remaining, the Knicks tried desperately to set up a game-tying play. However, a tough Indiana defense and poor execution on the part of the Knicks did not allow that to happen.

As the clock rolled to zero, Miller's eight points in nine seconds held, and the Pacers claimed victory.

"I'm in a state of disbelief," Pacers coach Larry Brown said. "We stole this game."

Miller's performance in Game 1 set the tone for a tight series. The teams were tied after six games, so it all came down to Game 7 in New York. With five seconds remaining, Ewing had a chance to tie the game. When his shot bounced off the rim and rolled out, the

Pacers had finally beaten the Knicks in a playoff series.

Behind Miller, the Pacers were consistently one of the top teams in the Eastern Conference during the 1990s. Their playoff battles with the Knicks became legendary. Many of the games and the series were close. But fans really loved watching the Midwestern Pacers go toe-to-toe with the big-city Knicks.

However, the Pacers' battles with the Knicks would often end up being the highlights of their playoff runs. After beating the Knicks in that historic Game 7 in the 1995 conference semifinals, the Pacers lost to the Orlando Magic in a seven-game conference final. Unfortunately for the Pacers and their fans, it was not the only time they fell just short during the 1990s.

REGGIE v. SPIKE

Pacers guard Reggie Miller did more than taunt the Knicks and their fans with his jump shot. He also taunted them with his words and actions. Perhaps his biggest adversary was Hollywood director and Knicks fan Spike Lee, who sits courtside at Madison Square Garden. The two often trash talked each other when Indiana played at New York.

During Game 5 of the 1994 Eastern Conference finals, the Knicks led the Pacers 70–58 after three quarters. Miller then scored 25 of his game-high 39 points in the fourth quarter as the Pacers won 93–86. During the run, Miller gestured to Lee by putting his hands around his neck to simulate choking. The image was splashed across New York's newspapers the next day and enflamed the rivalry even more.

"There's nothing I want more than to beat [the Knicks] on their stage, to steal their show," Miller said. "I got great enjoyment from it."

CHAPTER 2

AN ABA DYNASTY

Indiana was one of the first states to truly embrace basketball. Nearly every town and city, big or small, had a high school team it was crazy about. Many top college programs were in Indiana as well. So when the American Basketball Association (ABA) was founded in 1967 to challenge the NBA, it was a no-brainer that Indiana should have a professional team.

A group of 10 investors approached the ABA about bringing a team to Indianapolis, the state's capital and largest city. Their team, the Indiana Pacers, became one of the league's original 11 teams for the 1967–68 season.

For nine seasons, ABA teams dazzled fans with their flashy play and off-court gimmicks. And during that time, no team drew more fans or won more games than the Pacers.

The Pacers signed their first player, guard Roger Brown,

Center Mel Daniels starred for the Pacers from 1968–69 to 1973–74. He was the ABA MVP in 1968–69 and in 1970–71.

for $500. He would go on to become one of the most storied players to wear a Pacers uniform. And for their first coach, the Pacers hired Notre Dame assistant coach Larry Staverman.

A crowd of 10,835 people came to the Indiana State Fair Coliseum to see the Pacers' first game, even though the building only officially seated 9,111.

The First Great Player

Roger Brown had been banned from the NBA due to cheating, but that did not stop the ABA's Pacers from signing him in 1967. It was a good decision, as Brown averaged 17.4 points per game and was a four-time All-Star during his eight seasons in the ABA. Brown's success came despite his terrible eyesight. He often had to ask teammates how much time was left because he could not see the clock. However, since he had learned to shoot on the playgrounds of New York after dark, his poor eyesight had little impact on his shot.

The Pacers beat the Kentucky Colonels, 117–95. They went on to win their first five games, as well as 11 of their first 13 games. However, the first Pacers team finished only 38–40 and was swept in the first round of the playoffs.

The team wanted more. Staverman was fired early in their second season. Meanwhile, the Pacers set out to address their biggest weakness—size. Mel Daniels was one of the ABA's top big men. He played for the Minnesota Muskies in 1967–68. But when the Muskies ran into financial trouble, the Pacers offered to buy Daniels.

The teams initially signed a deal on a napkin. To get Daniels, the Pacers would give Minnesota two players, a first round pick, and $150,000. The Pacers ownership board, however, thought that was too

Pacers center Mel Daniels (34) reaches for a loose ball during a 1969 home game against the Kentucky Colonels.

steep a price. It came back with a new offer of $75,000 in addition to the players. In need of the money, the Muskies reluctantly agreed.

The move paid off for the Pacers. Daniels went on to become a two-time ABA Most Valuable Player (MVP), the fourth highest scorer in ABA history, and the ABA's all-time leader in rebounds.

Ten games into their second season, the Pacers also named former Indiana University and NBA star Bob "Slick" Leonard as coach. Leonard was known for his fiery personality. But he was able to turn the Pacers into a hardworking team that became known for its toughness.

"The Pacers were the bullies of the league," veteran ABA

Bob "Slick" Leonard coached the Pacers from 1968–69 until 1979–80. He guided them to three ABA championships.

guard Gene Littles said. "The only team I remember fighting with was Indiana."

With their new attitude, the Pacers improved to 44–34 in 1968–69. They averaged 119.6 points per game, a team record that still stood after the 2010–11 season. Daniels averaged 24 points and 16.5 rebounds per game and was the ABA MVP. The Pacers won the Eastern Division and beat the Colonels and the Miami Floridians to reach their first ABA Finals. However, they lost to the Oakland Oaks four games to one in the Finals.

The Pacers continued to improve in 1969–70. They won 59 games that season to take the Eastern Division by 14 games. In an April 12 game against the Pittsburgh Pipers, the Pacers set the all-time ABA mark for points in a game with 177. They cruised in the playoffs, losing only one game on the way to the Finals. And this time, they won. The Pacers beat the Los Angeles Stars four games to two to win their first ABA championship.

The Pacers got another boost before the 1971–72 season, when they signed 20-year-old George McGinnis. The 6-foot-8, 240-pound forward had starred at Indiana University, and he provided the Pacers with some much-needed youth.

With McGinnis's help, the Pacers marched to a 47–37 record in the regular season. Then they won two tight playoff series to advance to the ABA Finals. There, they beat the New York Nets in six games to clinch their second ABA

championship. The Pacers repeated as ABA champions in 1972–73, when they defeated the Colonels four games to three in the Finals. McGinnis was named the series MVP.

The Pacers were unable to match that success in following seasons. In 1974, they moved from the State Fair Coliseum to Market Square Arena, a 16,530-seat arena in downtown Indianapolis. They also traded an aging Daniels to the Memphis Sounds.

McGinnis truly became the Pacers' go-to player after that.

THE ABA

To help attract fans, the ABA tried many gimmicks and innovations, some of which are still common in today's NBA. The ABA gave the sport the three-point line, the first professional slam-dunk contest, and a number of previously unknown players who would become stars. The league was also known for its red, white, and blue ball. Still, the upstart league was rarely on national television and did not generate much national media attention. The ABA collapsed in 1976, but the following year, 10 of the NBA's 24 All-Stars were former ABA players.

"The ABA was like basketball's Wild West, and Julius Erving, George Gervin, James Silas, and all the other ABA stars were the gunfighters," said broadcaster Bob Costas, who got his start broadcasting the ABA's Spirits of St. Louis. "They are men of legend known to millions, but whose actual deeds were seen by few."

In 1974–75, he led them to a 45–39 record and back to the ABA Finals. However, the Pacers fell to the Colonels in five games. They would not reach another Finals for 25 years.

Although the Pacers had been a success during the ABA's first eight seasons, the ABA itself was never a strong league. Through the 1975–76 season, several ABA teams had either relocated or collapsed. The more established NBA decided to offer four ABA teams an opportunity to join the NBA. They were the Denver Nuggets, the New York Nets, the San Antonio Spurs, and the Indiana Pacers.

There was a catch, though. Each of the four ABA teams was required to pay the NBA $3.2 million. The ABA teams also could not receive money from television contracts for three seasons,

Pacers forward George McGinnis sets the ball into the basket during a 1975 game at Market Square Arena in Indianapolis.

participate in the 1976 college player draft, nor have any say in how the league divided ticket revenue for two years. The four ABA teams did get to keep their players, but the remaining ABA players were to be dispersed in a draft among NBA teams.

With the ABA struggling, the teams had little choice but to take the deal. The Pacers joined the Nuggets, the Spurs, and the Nets in the NBA for the 1976–77 season. Their previous ABA success, however, did not follow.

CHAPTER 3

IN THE NBA

C oach Bob "Slick" Leonard stayed in charge when the team joined the NBA in 1976–77. However, star forward George McGinnis had left the previous season. Guard Billy Knight led the Pacers with 26.6 points per game. Still, the team finished only 36–46 and fifth in the Midwest Division.

The Pacers weren't just short on wins; they were also short on money. Each of the surviving ABA teams owed $3.2 million to the NBA. They also owed money to two ABA teams as part of a settlement agreement, because those teams were not allowed to join the NBA.

In July 1977, the Pacers were at a crossroads. If season ticket sales for the 1977–78 season did not exceed 8,000 tickets by the end of the month, the owners announced that they would have to sell the team. And a new ownership group might move the team out of

Pacers guard John Williamson puts up a shot against the New York Nets during a 1977 game.

Indiana. In an effort to save the team, a "Save the Pacers" drive was held on the local WISH-8 TV to sell more season tickets.

The 16 1/2-hour telethon began on July 3, 1977. It aimed to remind fans that the Pacers were the pro basketball team that represented hundreds of small-town teams from across the state. On July 4, 10 minutes before the telethon was over, Leonard stood in front of the television cameras with his wife Nancy. They announced that the goal had been met.

"I knew if we didn't meet our goal, we probably wouldn't ever get another team back," Nancy Leonard told the *Indianapolis Star*.

The telethon not only helped keep the team in Indiana, it also helped reignite fan interest in the team all across the state. The Pacers' average attendance at Market Square Arena jumped from 7,615 in 1976–77 to 10,982 in the 1977–78 season. However, the increased fan support did not help the Pacers improve on the court. The team posted a 31–51 regular season mark, going 2–15 during one stretch of the year.

But improvement soon followed. The Pacers won 38 and then 37 games in the next two seasons. California millionaire Sam Nassi purchased the Pacers at the end of the 1978–79 season. Looking to recapture

The Pacers' Ricky Sobers makes a no-look pass during a 1978 game against the Kansas City Kings. It was one of 51 losses for the Pacers that season.

some of their old magic, the Pacers made a big move in 1979–80. They traded young forward Alex English and a first-round draft pick to the Denver Nuggets for former Pacers star McGinnis.

The move backfired. English became a star for the Nuggets. Meanwhile, McGinnis only played two and a half more seasons, never regaining his old form.

Following five straight losing seasons, Jack McKinney replaced Leonard as head coach in 1980–81. He guided the team to an 8–3 start and a 44–38 record. It was the Pacers' first winning record since joining the NBA. It was also good

SLICK LEONARD

Bob "Slick" Leonard grew up in a poor, working-class family in Terre Haute, Indiana. As a child, it was his responsibility to walk along the railroad tracks near his home in search of coal that had fallen off the train cars. His family used the coal to heat its house.

Leonard was a star high school basketball player in Terre Haute. He later played at Indiana University and then in the NBA with the Minneapolis/Los Angeles Lakers and the Chicago Packers/Zephyrs.

When Leonard took over the Pacers in 1969, he brought a blue-collar attitude and a tough, aggressive style. He also stressed team unity. Leonard won 529 games while coaching the Pacers for 12 years in the ABA and NBA. He later became known for his trademark phrase, "Boom, baby!" that he said each time a Pacers player hit a three-pointer while he served as the team's radio and TV broadcaster.

enough to get them into the NBA playoffs for the first time. The Philadelphia 76ers swept them in two games. However, McKinney was named NBA Coach of the Year.

The Pacers struggled to build upon that success, though. McKinney's structured offense did not mesh well with McGinnis's talents. In his second full year with McKinney, McGinnis's scoring average dropped from 13.1 to 4.7 points per game. McGinnis retired after the Pacers finished 35–47 that season.

"It hurt to see George play at the end, because he had meant so much to the team," former Pacers teammate Billy Keller said. "The shame is that the George McGinnis at the end of his career is the image people have of him, and that wasn't George. For years, he carried this team like no

Forward Clark Kellogg played five seasons with the Pacers, beginning in 1982–83. He led the team in scoring in each of his first three seasons.

other one player ever did before or after. That is how I'll always remember him."

The bright spot for the Pacers that season was rookie center Herb Williams. He grabbed 605 rebounds that year. The following year, the Pacers drafted his former Ohio State teammate, forward Clark Kellogg. However, Williams and

Kellogg could not lead the team to success. The Pacers finished last in the Central Division in each of the next four years. They finished a franchise-worst 20–62 in 1982–83.

In the spring of 1983, Nassi looked into selling the team to buyers in California. However, he ultimately found a buyer in shopping center moguls Melvin and Herbert Simon, who kept the team in Indianapolis.

In 1983–84, Kellogg averaged 19.1 points and 9.1 rebounds. Williams added 14.9 points and eight rebounds per game. But the Pacers finished only 26–56, and McKinney was let go at the end of the season. Pacers assistant George Irvine took over as head coach.

Things got worse before they got better. The Pacers finished 22–60 and 26–56 during Irvine's only two seasons in charge. Then, on April 22, 1986, Pacers assistant coach Donnie Walsh was promoted to general manager. The move would change the fate of the Pacers organization forever.

Walsh hired experienced coach Jack Ramsey to replace Irvine. Then the Pacers drafted forward Chuck Person. He combined with former number two overall draft pick Wayman Tisdale and veterans Williams, John Long, and Vern Fleming to immediately turn the Pacers around. Indiana finished 41–41 and qualified for the playoffs for only the second time since joining the NBA.

The Pacers claimed their first victory in an NBA playoff game in a 96–87 win over the Atlanta Hawks. However, they were still eliminated in the first round of the postseason.

Pacers forward Wayman Tisdale jumps to block a pass during a 1987 game against the Golden State Warriors.

This time, however, the Pacers were able to build upon their momentum. At the 1987 NBA Draft, many fans wanted Walsh to select former Indiana University star Steve Alford with the 11th overall pick. Instead, Walsh selected a skinny, 6-foot-7 guard from the University of California, Los Angeles, with a soft shooting touch and an instinct for scoring. His name was Reggie Miller.

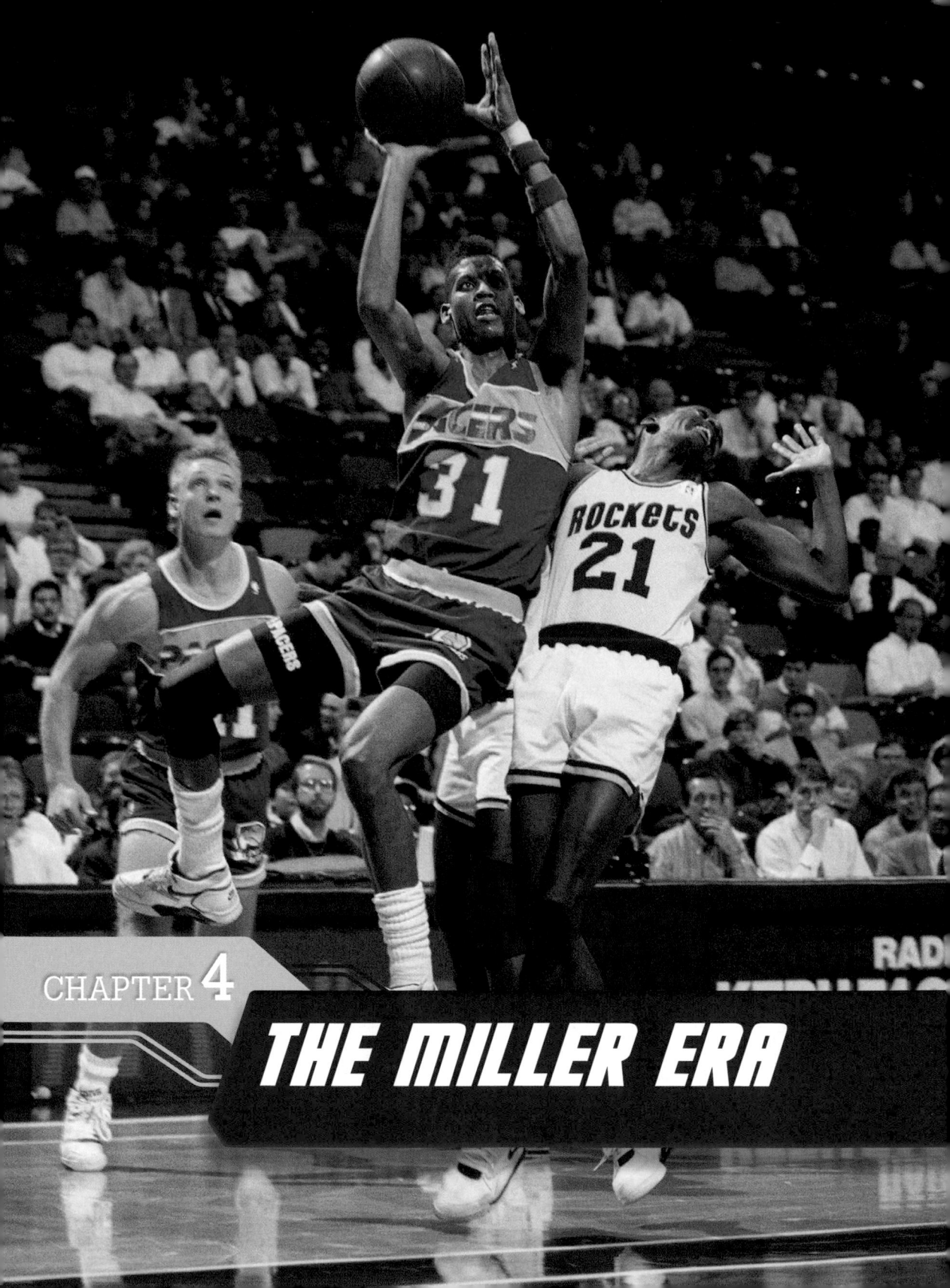

CHAPTER 4

THE MILLER ERA

Reggie Miller's storied career with the Pacers did not get off to a blazing start. In fact, the shooting guard started just one game during his rookie year, in 1987–88. The Pacers weren't so hot as a team, either. They missed the playoffs for the 10th time in 12 years.

The Pacers then added another player in the 1988 NBA Draft who would go on to become a team icon. Rik Smits, a 7-foot-4 center, made the NBA's All-Rookie team that year. Yet the Pacers still managed only 28 wins and again missed the playoffs.

Miller and Smits finally led the Pacers to the playoffs in 1989–90. It was the first of four straight years of making it. But they struggled to find a winning formula once in the postseason, and were knocked out in the first round each time. So the Pacers made some changes.

Reggie Miller knocks the Houston Rockets' Sleepy Floyd out of the way as he puts up a shot during a 1990 game.

The Pacers' Antonio Davis throws down a jam against the Atlanta Hawks during the 1994 Playoffs. Indiana won four games to two.

General manager Donnie Walsh hired Larry Brown to coach the team in 1993–94. The Pacers also traded for forward Derrick McKey before the season. He combined with forwards Dale Davis, rookie Antonio Davis, and Smits to give Indiana a physical front-court. The Pacers' tough post play mirrored the hard-nosed Pacers teams from the ABA.

The new and improved Pacers went 47–35. Then they swept the Orlando Magic and upset the top-seeded Atlanta Hawks in the playoffs. That set up a series against the New York Knicks to determine the conference champion. After splitting the first four games, the teams headed back to New York for Game 5. The Pacers had only won two of their previous 33 games in New York. The situation served as motivation for the outspoken Miller.

"I relish situations like this," he said before the game. "We're going against the best team in the NBA; we're on national TV. You've got to love the pressure. This is what it's all about. You've got to love it. That's what basketball is all about."

Still, the Pacers entered the fourth quarter trailing 70–58. That is when Miller delivered the first of his memorable play-off performances against the Knicks. He scored 25 of his 39 points in the fourth quarter as the Pacers came back to win, 93–86. Miller went 8-for-9 shooting while making all five three-pointers he attempted in the fourth quarter. He outscored the entire Knicks team, 25–16, during that time.

Cheryl Miller

Reggie Miller starred for the Pacers for 18 seasons, but he might not have even been the best player in his own family. His older sister, Cheryl Miller, was one of the most dominant women's basketball players ever. She guided her Riverside Polytechnic High School team to a 132–4 record over her career, even scoring 105 points in a single game. Then she was a four-time All-American at the University of Southern California and led her team to two national championships. During Reggie Miller's games, opposing fans would often chant Cheryl's name, trying to tease the younger Miller about his abilities.

"Everything felt like it was in slow motion," Miller said. "You see plays before they happen, read defenses and know what your defender is going to do before he does it."

The game was the Pacers' first on primetime network TV, and it made Miller a national star. However, the magic soon faded as the Knicks won the final two games. Miller had a chance to give the Pacers a lead with 4.2 seconds left in Game 7, but he threw up an air ball.

The Pacers added veteran point guard and ex-Knick Mark Jackson for the 1994–95 season. He helped them finish 52–30 and win the Central Division. The Pacers got a chance for redemption when they met the Knicks in the second round of the playoffs. Following Miller's eight points in nine seconds in Game 1, the Pacers eventually won the series in seven games.

Once again, however, the Pacers' luck ran out in the Eastern Conference finals. Center Shaquille O'Neal led the Magic to victory over the Pacers in seven games.

Coach Brown had led the Pacers to the Eastern Conference finals in each of his first two seasons. That was the furthest the Pacers had advanced since joining the NBA in 1976–77. However, with Miller suffering an injury to his eye socket, the Pacers lost in the first round of the 1995–96 playoffs. More injuries plagued the Pacers during the next season. They went 39–43 and missed the playoffs for the first time in eight seasons. It would be the only season in which they fell short of the postseason between 1989–90 and 2005–06.

Brown took much of the blame for the team's struggles in 1995–96 and resigned. That

New York Knicks center Patrick Ewing guards the Pacers' Reggie Miller during the 1995 Eastern Conference finals.

opened the door for NBA legend and Indiana native Larry Bird to take over. Bird guided the team to 58 wins and back to the Eastern Conference finals in his first season.

Miller showed the playoff heroics he had become known for against Michael Jordan and the Chicago Bulls. On a

sprained ankle, he scored 13 of his 28 points in the final four minutes of Game 3. Then, in Game 4, he hit a three-pointer with 2.7 seconds left to give the

More than a Game

"In 49 states it's just basketball . . . but this is Indiana." —Video boards in Conseco Fieldhouse

Pacers a 96–94 victory. But in the end, the Pacers again lost in seven games.

A labor dispute cut the 1998–99 season short. The Pacers still managed a 33–17 record and again reached the Eastern Conference finals. This time, the eighth-seeded Knicks surprised the Pacers with a six-game defeat.

The Pacers had consistently been one of the better teams in the Eastern Conference throughout the 1990s. Yet after four attempts, they could not get past the conference finals. The team made some changes before the 1999–2000 season.

Indiana parted ways with Antonio Davis that off-season. The Pacers also moved into the brand new Conseco Fieldhouse.

The Dunking Dutchman

The Pacers made Rik Smits the second overall pick in the 1988 NBA Draft. He was never a superstar, but the giant center became a staple on the Pacers teams of the 1990s. Born in the Netherlands and known as "The Dunking Dutchman," Smits played all of his 12 NBA seasons with the Pacers. He made the All-Star team once, in 1998, but consistently averaged around 15 points and six rebounds per game.

The moves helped breathe fresh life into the team. Guard Jalen Rose had a breakout season, averaging 18.2 points per game. It was the first time in 11 seasons that Miller, who averaged 18.1 points per game, did not lead the Pacers in scoring.

The Pacers won 56 games and another division title in 1999–2000. The Milwaukee Bucks nearly upset them in the

Pacers center Rik Smits puts up a jumper against the New York Knicks during the 1998 playoffs.

first round of the playoffs, but a last-second basket in Game 5 sent Indiana through to the second round.

The Pacers beat their old coach, Brown, and the Philadelphia 76ers in the second round. Then they met the Knicks in the conference finals. It was the sixth time in eight years that the two teams met in the playoffs.

After the teams split the first four games, the Pacers were finally able to pull through. Guard Travis Best scored 24 points as Indiana won Game 5 by a score of 88–79. The Pacers closed out the series with a 93–80 win at Madison Square Garden in Game 6. Miller scored 17 of his 34 points in the fourth quarter.

"It's a great thing to happen to us," Bird said. "Our veteran players have been around the league and battled so hard over the years and never had an opportunity to play in the Finals and this is their day."

The Pacers had finally reached the NBA Finals. However, they met a dominant Los Angeles Lakers team when they got there. The Lakers featured league MVP O'Neal and promising young guard Kobe Bryant. The Pacers had no answer for O'Neal as the giant

Reggie Miller and the Pacers won Game 3 of the 2000 NBA Finals at home but lost the series to the Los Angeles Lakers in six games.

center averaged 38 points and nearly 17 rebounds per game. The Lakers eventually won the series in six games.

It was another disappointing ending to a season for Pacers fans. They had finally gotten to the NBA Finals, but through the 2010–11 season, it remained the closest the Pacers had been to an NBA championship.

CHAPTER 5

REBUILDING

A new era in Pacers basketball began in 2000–01. Larry Bird had resigned as coach and was replaced by former Indiana University and NBA star Isiah Thomas. The aging Pacers also lost several players who had helped them rise to prominence during the 1990s.

Starters Rik Smits, Mark Jackson, and Dale Davis, along with key contributor Chris Mullin, all left the team. Smits retired. Mullin was released. Jackson signed with the Toronto Raptors. Davis was traded to the Portland Trail Blazers for a raw young power forward named Jermaine O'Neal.

Guards Reggie Miller and Jalen Rose remained the stars of the Pacers. But they struggled to maintain their success from the previous season. Indiana finished 41–41 and lost in first round of the playoffs.

The Pacers had a 26–27 record more than halfway through the 2001–02 season.

Brad Miller, *left*, and Ron Artest, *right*, led a new generation of Pacers teams after joining during the 2001–02 season.

Looking to make a change, they traded Rose and others to the Chicago Bulls. In return, the Pacers received center Brad Miller, forward Ron Artest, and guards Kevin Ollie and Ron Mercer. The Pacers still finished only 42–40 and lost in the first round of the playoffs. But there were some signs of life in the new players.

O'Neal was emerging as a top power forward. He averaged 19 points and 10.5 rebounds per game, and made his first All-Star team in 2001–02. Artest was also establishing himself as a defensive force.

The Pacers appeared to be turning the corner during the 2002–03 season. Their 34–15 record at the All-Star break was the best in the Eastern Conference. O'Neal made his second straight All-Star game, and Brad Miller made his first. But the Pacers faded down the stretch, going 11–19 to end the season. They again fell in the first round of the playoffs.

More changes came after that season. Unable to afford Brad Miller, the Pacers traded him to the Sacramento Kings. Bird also rejoined the Pacers as team president. One of his first moves was firing Thomas and replacing him with Rick Carlisle.

Under Carlisle, the Pacers won a team-record 61 games. O'Neal made his third All-Star team and Artest was named the NBA's Defensive Player of the Year. The Pacers then marched back to the Eastern Conference finals, where they met the Detroit Pistons. It was the sixth conference finals appearance in 11 years for Indiana. However, like four of their previous tries, the Pacers lost.

Pacers' fans had high expectations going into the 2004–05

Jermaine O'Neal, *left*, and Reggie Miller celebrate after Miller hit a late three-pointer to secure a victory during the 2004 playoffs.

season. A game against the Pistons on November 19, 2004, changed that. The Pacers had a 97–82 lead with 45.9 seconds left when Artest fouled Pistons center Ben Wallace hard as he went up for a layup. The benches quickly emptied and chaos broke out on the floor. Artest, who had a history of suspensions, tried to remove himself from the situation.

But when a fan threw a cup of soda on him, Artest ran into the stands and began throwing punches. Pacers teammate Stephen Jackson followed Artest into the stands. Later, after the game had been called, Artest and O'Neal punched fans who had come onto the court.

Two days after the brawl, nine players between the two teams were suspended for more than 140 total games. Artest was suspended for the season. Jackson was suspended for 30 games and O'Neal for 25, although his suspension was eventually reduced to 15.

The suspensions left the Pacers with a shell of their usual roster. But they rallied behind 39-year-old Reggie Miller. He led them back to the playoffs and to an upset over the Boston Celtics in the first round. But they eventually lost to the Pistons in the second round. Miller scored 27 points in an 88–79 loss

to the Pistons in what would be his final game.

Miller's retirement marked the end of an era in Pacers basketball. The Pacers had five straight non-winning seasons following his retirement. Artest demanded a trade during the 2005–06 season, adding to the team's struggles. Then the following season, Carlisle left after the team finished 35–47 and missed the playoffs for the first time in 10 years.

A new era began the next season under new coach Jim O'Brien. Young forward Danny Granger enjoyed a breakout season, averaging 19.6 points per game. He would soon establish himself as the new face of the team. However, the Pacers finished only 36–46 and missed the playoffs again.

The turnover continued. Longtime general manager Donnie Walsh left near the end

Danny Granger prepares to make a move against the Pacers' old nemesis, the New York Knicks, during a 2011 game.

of the 2007–08 season. Bird replaced him and traded away a declining O'Neal. Granger averaged a career-high 25.8 points per game in 2008–09. But the Pacers continued to struggle and again missed the playoffs in 2008–09 and 2009–10.

When Indiana started the 2010–11 season 17–27, O'Brien was fired. The Pacers finished the season 37–45 under new coach Frank Vogel and returned to the playoffs as the eighth seed. However, the powerful Chicago Bulls eliminated them in the first round.

Despite the early playoff exit, the Pacers' core of young players—such as center Roy Hibbert, point guard Darren Collison, and Granger—gave fans hope that their team will soon return to the NBA's elite.

TIMELINE

1967	The Indiana Pacers defeat the Kentucky Colonels in their first ABA game on October 14 at the Indiana State Fair Coliseum.
1968	The Pacers hire Bob "Slick" Leonard to coach the team. Leonard guides the Pacers to three ABA championships and 529 career wins during his career.
1970	The Pacers defeat the Los Angeles Stars in six games to win their first ABA championship.
1972	The Pacers defeat the New York Nets in six games to win the ABA Finals.
1972	George McGinnis sets the Pacers' single-game scoring record with 58 points against the Dallas Chaparrals (now the San Antonio Spurs) on November 28.
1973	The Pacers win their third ABA championship in four years when they defeat Kentucky in seven games. Through 2010–11, it was their last championship.
1974	The Pacers move into Market Square Arena.
1976	The NBA agrees to merge with four remaining ABA teams, including the Pacers.
1976	The Pacers play their first NBA game against the Boston Celtics on October 21 at Market Square Arena, but lose 129–122 in overtime.
1986	Donnie Walsh becomes the Pacers general manager. He goes on to build the talented Pacers teams of the 1990s.

 **1987**	The Pacers select Reggie Miller with the 11th overall pick in the 1987 NBA Draft.
1994	Miller becomes a national star on June 1, shocking New York City by scoring 25 points in the fourth quarter of Game 5 of the Eastern Conference finals against the New York Knicks. He taunts Knicks fan Spike Lee in the process.
1995	Miller scores eight points in nine seconds on May 7 to overcome the Knicks in Game 1 of the Eastern Conference semifinals.
 **1995**	The Pacers defeat their archrivals, the Knicks, for the first time in a playoff series.
1999	The Pacers move into Conseco Fieldhouse.
2000	The Pacers advance to their first NBA Finals by beating the Knicks in the Eastern Conference finals. However, they lose to the Los Angeles Lakers in the NBA Finals.
 **2004**	The brawl at the Palace of Auburn Hills on November 19 results in nine player suspensions for more than 140 games between the Pacers and the Detroit Pistons.
2005	Miller scores 27 points in his final game. He played all of his 18 NBA seasons with the Pacers.
2011	After the Pacers start 17–27, coach Jim O'Brien is fired and replaced by Frank Vogel. The Pacers finish 37–45 and return to the playoffs for the first time since 2005–06, but lose to the Chicago Bulls in the first round.

QUICK STATS

FRANCHISE HISTORY

Indiana Pacers (1967–)

NBA FINALS
(1977 –)

2000

ABA FINALS
(1968–76; wins in bold)

1969, **1970**, **1972**, **1973**, 1975

CONFERENCE FINALS
(1977 –)

1994, 1995, 1998, 1999, 2000, 2004

KEY PLAYERS
(position[s]; years with team)

Roger Brown (F; 1967–74, 1975)
Mel Daniels (C; 1968–74)
Antonio Davis (F/C; 1993–99)
Dale Davis (F; 1991–2000, 2005)
Danny Granger (F; 2005–)
Billy Knight (G; 1974–77, 1979–83)
George McGinnis (F; 1971–75, 1980–82)
Reggie Miller (G; 1987–2005)
Jermaine O'Neal (F/C; 2000–08)
Jalen Rose (G; 1996–2002)
Rik Smits (C; 1988–2000)

KEY COACHES

Bob "Slick" Leonard (1968–80): 529–456; 69–47 (postseason)
Larry Brown (1993–97): 190–138; 22–16 (postseason)
Larry Bird (1997–2000): 147–67; 32–20 (postseason)

HOME ARENAS

Indiana State Fair Coliseum (1967–74)
Market Square Arena (1974–99)
Conseco Fieldhouse (1999–)

* All statistics through 2010–11 season

QUOTES AND ANECDOTES

During the 1974–75 season, Pacers forward George McGinnis was perhaps the ABA's best player. He shared the ABA MVP Award with Julius Erving, nicknamed Dr. J. However, McGinnis averaged more points (29.8), rebounds (14.3), and assists (6.3) than the now famous Dr. J (27.9 points, 10.9 rebounds, 5.5 assists).

By the time he came to the Pacers as a coach in 1993, Larry Brown had already coached every other ABA team that had merged into the NBA (the Spurs, the Nets, the Nuggets, and now the Pacers). Brown had coached eight different college and professional teams in the 21 years before joining the Pacers.

"I'm excited about the opportunity to work with the players Donnie's assembled," Brown said of Pacers general manager Donnie Walsh. "I'm hopeful this will be my last stop."

It was not. After being fired by the Pacers, Brown coached the Philadelphia 76ers, the Detroit Pistons, the New York Knicks, and the Charlotte Bobcats until being fired by Charlotte during the 2010–11 season.

The Pacers have two mascots. Boomer is a cat, and Bowser is a dog.

"In Reggie's mind, there was no bigger platform; this was his mission in life, he wanted Indiana to beat the Knicks." —Cheryl Miller, on her brother Reggie Miller's desire to beat the archrival New York Knicks

GLOSSARY

archrival

The opponent that brings out the greatest emotion in a team, its fans, and its players.

assist

A pass that leads directly to a made basket.

attendance

The number of fans at a particular game or who come to watch a team play during a particular season.

contract

A binding agreement about, for example, years of commitment by a basketball player in exchange for a given salary.

draft

A system used by professional sports leagues to select new players in order to spread incoming talent among all teams. The NBA Draft is held each June.

expansion

In sports, the addition of a franchise or franchises to a league.

franchise

An entire sports organization, including the players, coaches, and staff.

general manager

The executive who is in charge of the team's overall operation. He or she hires and fires coaches, drafts players, and signs free agents.

merge

Combine together.

postseason

The games in which the best teams play after the regular-season schedule has been completed.

rebound

To secure the basketball after a missed shot.

rookie

A first year player in the NBA.

telethon

A fundraiser that is broadcasted on television.

FOR MORE INFORMATION

Further Reading

Brunner, Conrad. *Boom Baby!: The Sudden, Surprising Rise of the Indiana Pacers.* Indianapolis: Masters Press, 1994.

Miller, Reggie. *I Love Being the Enemy: A Season on the Court with the NBA's Best Shooter and Sharpest Tongue.* New York: Simon & Schuster, 1995.

Simmons, Bill. *The Book of Basketball: The NBA According to the Sports Guy.* New York: Random House, 2009.

Web Links

To learn more about the Indiana Pacers, visit ABDO Publishing Company online at **www.abdopublishing.com**. Web sites about the Pacers are featured on our Book Links page. These links are routinely monitored and updated to provide the most current information available.

Places to Visit

Conseco Fieldhouse
125 South Pennsylvania Street
Indianapolis, IN 46204
317-917-2727
www.consecofieldhouse.com
This has been the Pacers' home arena since 1999. Tours are available when the Pacers are not playing.

**Indiana Basketball
Hall of Fame**
408 Trojan Lane
New Castle, IN 47362
765-529-1891
www.hoopshall.com
This hall of fame highlights the rich history of basketball in the state of Indiana. Indiana basketball legends and Pacers legends are enshrined here.

**Naismith Memorial
Basketball Hall of Fame**
1000 West Columbus Avenue
Springfield, MA 01105
413-781-6500
www.hoophall.com
This hall of fame and museum highlights the greatest players and moments in the history of basketball. Adrian Dantley, Alex English, and Gus Johnson are among the former Pacers enshrined here.

INDEX

About the Author

Josh Fowler is a journalist who has written for print, radio, and television. He has covered major college football, basketball, and volleyball teams, NASCAR events, and national breaking news as a television reporter and producer. His love for basketball blossomed while growing-up in Lafayette, Indiana, watching Reggie Miller and the Pacers with his dad. He currently works in communications for a Fortune 500 company and lives in Bloomington, Illinois, with his wife.